Contents

Introduction   6

Journey map   8

On a coral island   10

The reef flat   12

The reef crest   14

Amongst the coral   16

Going deeper   18

The reef at night   20

Down the slope   22

Inside a Coral Reef

Carole Telford and

Rod Theodorou

Heinemann
LIBRARY

First published in Great Britain by Heinemann Library

Halley Court, Jordan Hill, Oxford OX2 8EJ,

a division of Reed Educational and Professional Publishing Ltd.

OXFORD FLORENCE PRAGUE MADRID ATHENS

MELBOURNE AUCKLAND KUALA LUMPUR SINGAPORE TOKYO

IBADAN NAIROBI KAMPALA JOHANNESBURG GABORONE

PORTSMOUTH NH (USA) CHICAGO MEXICO CITY SAO PAULO

© Reed Educational and Professional Publishing Ltd 1997

Designed by Aricot Vert Design Ltd

Illustrations by Stephen Lings and Jane Pickering at Linden Artists

Printed and bound in China

01 00 99 98

10 9 8 7 6 5 4 3 2 1

ISBN 0 431 05553 X

British Library Cataloguing in Publication Data

Theodorou, Rod

Inside a Coral Reef. – (Amazing Journeys)

1. Coral reef ecology – Juvenile literature 2. Coral reefs and islands – Juvenile literature

I. Title II. Telford, Carole, 1961–

577.7'89

Acknowledgements

The Publishers would like to thank the following for permission to reproduce photographs:

Ardea (D. Parer and E. Parer-Cook) pp. 6, 17 (top), 26, (Mike Osmond) p. 25 (top), (Ron and Valerie Taylor) pp. 13 (bottom), 14, 19 (bottom), 21 (bottom), 24, (Valerie Taylor) p. 25 (bottom), (A.D. Trounson and M.C. Clampett) p. 15 (bottom), (A. Warren) p. 11 (top); FLPA (C. Carvalho) p. 23 (bottom), (D. Fleetham/Silvestris) p. 27, (T. and P. Gardner) p. 10; NHPA (Cyril Webster) p. 15 (top), (Bill Wood) p. 20; OSF (Fred Bavendam) pp. 19 (top), 21 (top), 23 (top), (David B. Fleetham) p. 17 (bottom), (Babs and Bert Wells) p. 11 (bottom), (Norbert Wu) p. 13 (top).

Cover photograph: Oxford Scientific Films

Our thanks to Rob Alcraft for his comments in the preparation of this book.

Every effort has been made to contact copyright holders of any material reproduced in this book. Any omissions will be rectified in subsequent printings if notice is given to the Publisher.

The drop-off   24

Conservation and the future   26

Glossary   28

Further reading and addresses   30

Index   32

Some words are shown in bold letters, **like this**. You can find out what these words mean by looking in the Glossary.

Introduction

You are about to go on an amazing journey. You are going to visit one of the greatest natural wonders of the world: the Great Barrier Reef. This is the largest of all coral reefs, stretching for over 2000 kilometres around the north-east coast of Australia. It is made by tiny little animals called corals.

You will begin your journey on the hot, dry sands of a coral island. You will then enter the warm, shallow waters of the reef and swim into a wonderful underwater garden of colours. On your way you will see some of the 5000 **species** of animals and plants that make their home in this amazing world.

This photo was taken from an aeroplane. It shows one of the many reefs that make up the Great Barrier Reef.

Reefs are made by tiny sea creatures called coral polyps. Polyps are tiny soft-bodied animals, smaller than a match head. Each polyp builds a small rocky **skeleton** around itself. When it dies the skeleton is left behind. Other polyps build their skeletons on top of it. Over thousands of years, millions of these skeletons form huge, rocky reefs. Scientists think the Great Barrier Reef began forming over 30 million years ago.

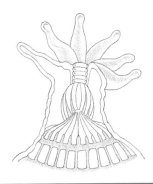

Coral polyp

Lots of fish and other sea creatures eat the polyps and find places to hide amongst the coral. More animals live amongst coral reefs than anywhere else in the oceans.

Coral reefs grow in warm seas all over the world.

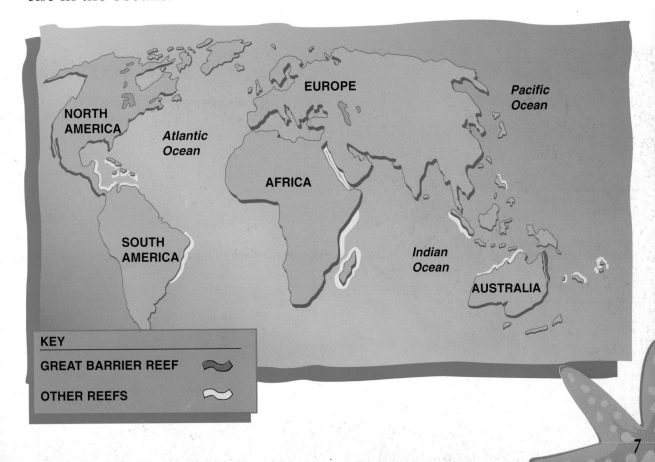

EUROPE

Pacific Ocean

NORTH AMERICA

Atlantic Ocean

AFRICA

SOUTH AMERICA

Indian Ocean

AUSTRALIA

KEY

GREAT BARRIER REEF

OTHER REEFS

Journey map

Coral island

Page 10

Beach

Page 12

Reef flat

Here is a map of our journey. We start on a coral island, which has been made by **fragments** of broken coral being pushed by waves onto a high part of the reef. An island like this takes thousands of years to form. In front of the island is a shallow stretch of water called the **reef flat**, ending at the **reef crest**. Beyond that we shall swim down the outer slopes of the reef where most of the corals and other sea creatures live.

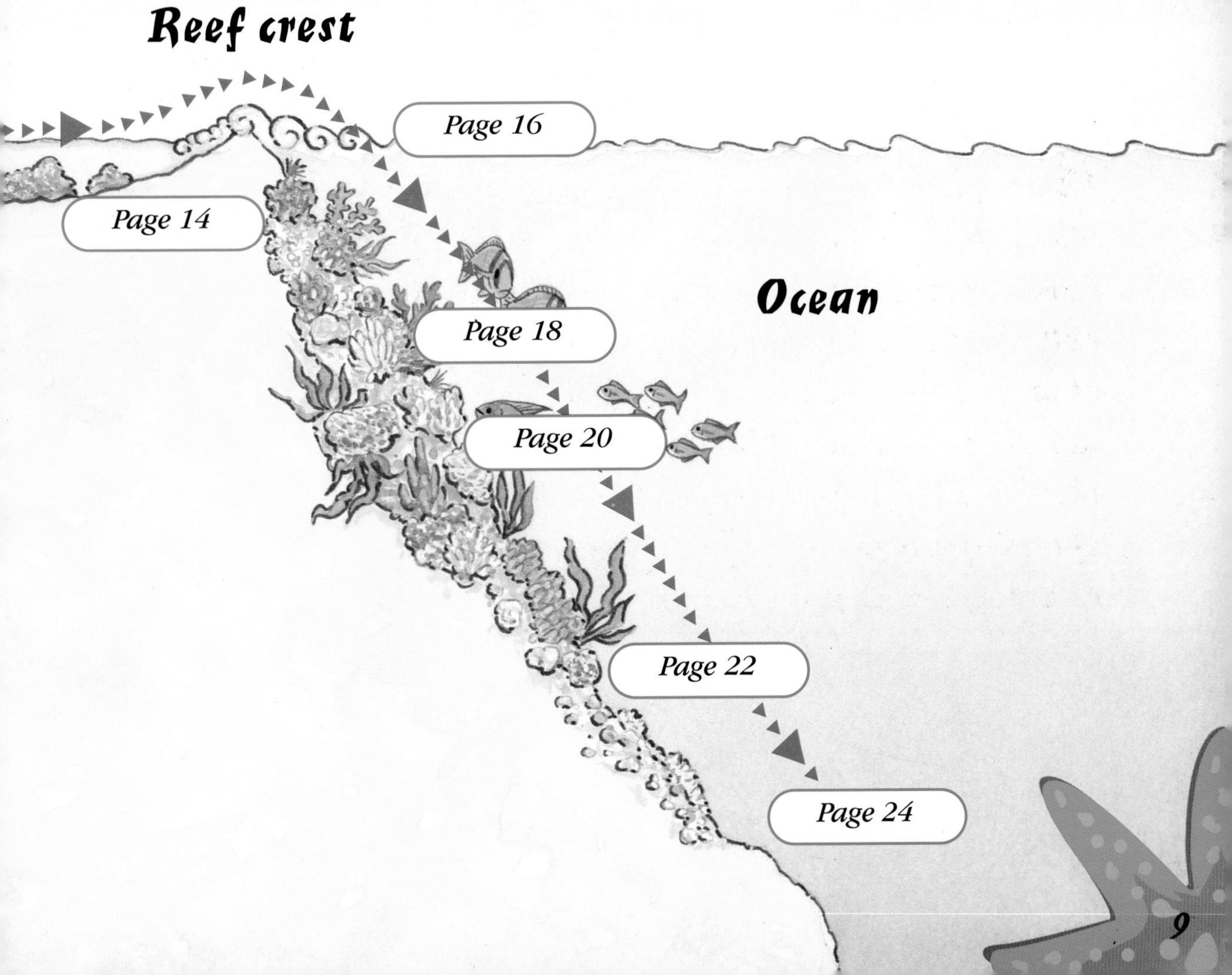

Reef crest

Page 16

Page 14

Ocean

Page 18

Page 20

Page 22

Page 24

On a coral island

We are standing on the hot, white sand of a coral island. The fierce summer sun beats down on our necks. It is always hot here, even in the middle of winter. If we scoop up a handful of sand and look at it closely we see it is made of tiny **fragments** of coral and shell.

Birds hurry out of our way. Many are looking for the worms that live in the sand. Some search the beach for washed-up jellyfish and other dead creatures. Behind us, past the sand dunes, bushes and trees, are thousands of nesting birds, filling the air with their noisy squawks.

This is Heron Island.
There are thousands of coral islands, called cays, in the Great Barrier Reef.

White-breasted sea eagle

This large bird snatches fish from the surface of the sea and steals chicks from other birds' nests. Because of people visiting coral islands and disturbing these birds, they are now quite **rare**.

White-capped noddy

This beautiful bird makes ugly, untidy nests in trees, but its droppings make the soil richer. It also carries seeds of other trees to the island.

Green turtles

Once a year female green turtles come onto the beach to dig holes and lay their eggs. Two or three months later the baby turtles hatch and crawl towards the sea. Many are eaten by **predators**.

The reef flat

Time for a swim! We wade into the water and swim out into the **reef flat**. The water here is only about a metre deep and very warm. It is a difficult place for coral to live. At **low tide** there is a chance that the coral will be left in the open air and dry out. This would kill most types of coral, which need to stay under water to survive.

However, some corals do manage to live and grow here. They form little coral islands on the sandy sea bed. Many creatures live in the warm, shallow water among them. We must be careful not to step on stingrays, which hide in the sand. They have sharp, poisonous **barbs** on their tails.

jelly fish

angel fish

parrot fish

spiny lobster

brittle star

wrasse

sea urchin

star fish

crab

cowrie

sponges

Mantis shrimp

This beautifully coloured shrimp is a fierce hunter and fighter. It is only about 15cm long, but can shoot its **pincers** forward so fast they can smash open a crab's shell.

Sea cucumber

These strange animals crawl over the coral on rows of little feet. They have **tentacles** at one end of their body, which they use to catch tiny floating sea creatures to eat.

Sea snails

Many sea snails live on the reef flat. The hard shells protect the soft creatures inside from being eaten. They move slowly over the coral feeding off the **algae** growing there.

The reef crest

As we reach the edge of the **reef flat** we can see the white foam of waves, breaking against the **reef crest**. This is where the top of the reef meets the open sea. As waves crash against the reef crest, they break off the coral and wash it over into the reef flat. There is a lot of broken coral lying around here. Storms will break off even more.

At first we cannot see any signs of life. Can anything live in this wild place? Then we spot some giant limpets clinging to the rocks. Even the biggest waves cannot knock them off. Each has a 'foot' which sucks it onto the rocks. At **low tide** they crawl over the rock eating **algae**.

More than 7cm across, these giant limpets can cling on to the rocks, despite the crashing waves at high tide.

Hermit crab

This small crab lives inside empty shells. It comes out to feed on dead animals thrown up onto the rubble at the reef crest. When it grows too big for its shell it simply finds a new, larger shell to crawl into.

Reef heron

At low tide the reef heron may wade along the rocky reef crest looking for prey in the water below. It uses its long, sharp beak to stab fish or shrimp.

Stonefish

Piles of rock and broken coral make a good hiding place for the stonefish. It waits amongst the rocks for smaller fish to come near enough for it to gobble them up. Stepping on a stonefish can be very painful. It has poisonous spines on its back to protect it from **predators**.

Amongst the coral

We are swimming away from the crest downwards along a gentle slope. The water is calmer and warm. Many different types of coral can grow here, safe from the crashing waves above. There are two groups of coral: 'hard' and 'soft'. We can see hard corals such as brain coral. These are the corals which leave the rocky **skeletons** behind that build the reef. Soft corals do not make these hard, rocky shells. They grow upwards in a mass of delicate branches that reach out into the water. They are also the most colourful of all the corals.

There are over 400 species of coral on the reef. It is hard to believe that each one is a community of millions of tiny animals.

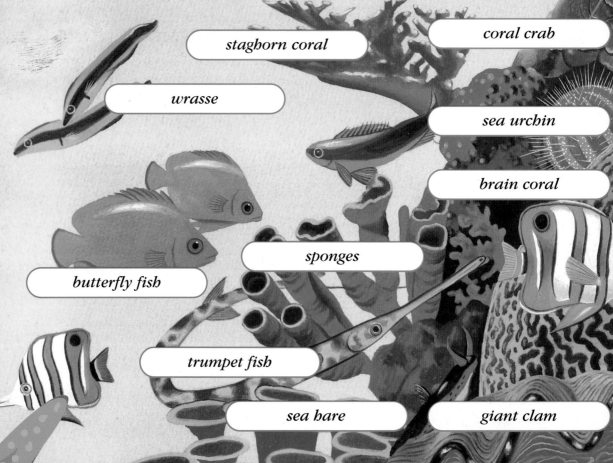

sea horses

coral crab

staghorn coral

wrasse

sea urchin

brain coral

sponges

butterfly fish

trumpet fish

sea hare

giant clam

Giant clam

The giant clam is a huge animal that can grow up to 1.4 metres wide! It lives on the reef, sucking water in to **filter** out **zooplankton** which it eats. This clam is sending out a cloud of eggs.

Gorgonian coral

This beautiful soft coral grows in a great fan that sways in the current. Like all corals it eats zooplankton. Each coral polyp catches the zooplankton with its tiny **tentacles**.

Cleaner wrasse

This fish gets its food in an unusual way. Other fish let the wrasse nibble around their mouth and **gills**. The wrasse picks off **parasites** and cleans the fish, helping it to stay healthy. In return the wrasse gets a meal!

Going deeper

We continue to swim down amongst the corals. Sunlight filters down through the water, so we can still see clearly. **Anemones** wave their beautiful but stinging **tentacles** in the current. Bright flashes of colour dart away as we swim. These are **shoals** of fish that live on the reef. Their narrow shape helps them slip easily between the coral to escape being eaten. Many are brightly coloured with stripes and spots. This makes them harder to see when they swim amongst the colourful coral. We see the long, black shape of a moray eel as it twists back into a hole.

branching coral

reef shark

star fish

sponges

wrasse

clown fish

moray eel

anemones

coral shrimp

trigger fish

Clown fish

Anemones catch fish with their stinging tentacles. The clown fish covers itself with a special slime that protects it from the stings. It lives among the tentacles, eating the leftovers from the anemone's meals.

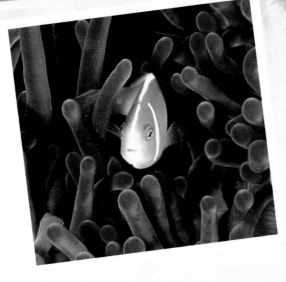

Trumpet fish

This strange fish hides behind big plant-eating fish. When smaller fish come close, it suddenly shoots forward and eats them. Then it hides among branching coral with its tail up in the water so it is **camouflaged** from **predators**.

Moray eel

This large hunter can squeeze and twist through holes and small spaces to chase out smaller, sleepy fish.

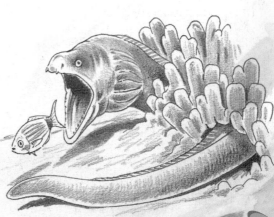

The reef at night

We have returned to the reef at night. The water is colder. There is nothing but darkness all around us. It is a strange feeling. The reef looks very different, lit by the beams of our underwater torches. Many of the fish we saw during the day are sleeping. They are hidden in the holes and cracks between the rocks.

Some fish come out only at night. The light from our torch catches a soldier fish in its beam. It quickly swims away. It will hide amongst the coral until it feels safe to come out and feed on **plankton**. The corals are even more colourful at night. Many of the coral polyps open out to feed in the darkness. There is less risk of a hungry fish biting off their **tentacles**.

At night our torches light up a mass of colourful feeding coral polyps.

20

Crown of thorns

This large starfish feeds at
night on the coral polyps.
It can destroy large areas
of reef. Its arms are
covered with poisonous,
sharp spines that protect
it from being eaten.

Soldier fish

The soldier fish is a small fish with
large eyes that help it to see at night.
It hides in caves during the day, and
feeds on **plankton** at night when it
is safer.

Lion fish

This beautiful lion fish is covered
with poisonous spines. It comes out
at nighi and swims slowly through
the reef looking for sleeping fish
to attack.

Down the slope

It is daytime again, and we are diving deeper down the sloping reef front. It is harder for the sun's light to reach down here. We can see different **species** of coral that can live in this gloomy light. As we swim deeper and deeper, we see more and more sponges. At last there are no corals growing. It is simply too dark for them to grow at this depth. The current is strong here, and the water is colder. Turning away from the coral we look out into the open sea. There are dark shadows moving out there.

green turtle

sharks

potato cod

butterfly fish

wrasse

biscuit starfish

sponges

moray eel

octopus

White-tip sharks

These greyish-brown sharks swim around the gloomy reef edge, then dart in amongst the fish to attack. They look frightening, but, like most sharks, white-tips never attack people.

Sponges

Sponges look like plants but are actually animals. They suck water in and out of holes to **filter zooplankton**. Many types of sponge live on reefs, including these large barrow sponges.

Potato cod

These huge fish (sometimes called groupers) can grow up to 2 m long. All potato cod are born females. They change into males when they grow to full size.

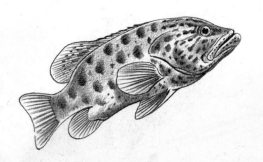

The drop-off

We have reached the end of the reef which is like a cliff edge. Below us is nothing but blackness. A few sponges grow on the cliff sides, but there is no living coral. Around us is the dark, cold world of the open ocean. We see a strange bat-like shadow gliding above us. It is a huge manta ray, attracted by the bubbles from our breathing apparatus. Long silver barracuda pass slowly by, hunting for fish. It is time to return to the surface.

Manta rays suck in water through their huge mouths to filter out plankton.

Sea snake

These poisonous snakes have flattened tails to help them swim. They come to the surface to breathe air but can then swim deep into the ocean, holding their breath for as long as eight hours!

Humpback whale →

Each year humpback whales make the long journey from the cold Antarctic to the warm waters of the Great Barrier Reef to breed. Adults grow up to 15 m long and communicate with squeals and moans called whale song.

Barracuda

These big, fierce fish grow up to 2 m long and have teeth like spears. They usually hunt in packs. Sometimes a single barracuda will follow a scuba-diver for some time, but they very rarely attack.

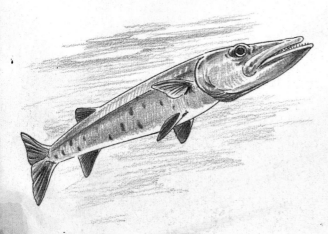

Conservation and the future

The Great Barrier Reef, along with other coral reefs in the world, is in danger. Storms cause some damage, but most threats come from people. Pollution from farming, industry, and shipping can poison the coral polyps. Fishermen and divers kill fish and gather corals and shells to sell to tourists. The crown of thorns starfish is usually attacked and eaten by the giant triton shell, pufferfish, and triggerfish. But many of these **predators** have been killed by humans, allowing the starfish to grow in numbers. Now thousands of these starfish are destroying huge stretches of reef.

A cyclone has devastated this reef. It will take many years to grow again.

Protecting the reef

As we learn more about coral reefs, we realize that most kinds of sea animal feed on other animals. By robbing the reef of coral, shells or fish, we can do terrible damage. The Great Barrier Reef Marine Park Authority now has rules about how the reef is used, to protect it from damage. They stop people harming the reef and study the effects of pollution on the coral polyps. By learning more about the fascinating world of the coral reef, we can understand how to protect these amazing places for many years to come.

The Great Barrier Reef Marine Park is a huge area of reef that is protected for the future.

Glossary

algae	very small plants that live in water
anemone	soft, jelly-like animal
barbs	sharp hooks
camouflaged	coloured or shaped in a way that makes an animal hard to see
dune	hill made when sand is blown about
filter	to sieve out
fragments	tiny broken pieces
gills	parts of a fish that let it get oxygen from water
low tide	the point when the sea is furthest from the beach
parasites	an animal or plant that lives in or on other plants and animals
pincer	a gripping claw
plankton	tiny plants and animals that live drifting in ocean currents
predator	an animal that hunts and kills other animals for food
rare	not very many are left
reef crest	rocky edge of the reef flat, where the reef meets the sea
reef flat	shallow part of a reef

shoal   group of fish swimming together for safety

skeleton   hard frame for a soft body

species   a group of living things that are very similar

tentacle   soft part of coral, which bends and feels for food

zooplankton   tiny creatures that are eaten by coral polyps

Further reading and addresses

Books

A Field Guide to the Coral Reef Fishes of the Indian and western Pacific Oceans, R.H. Carcasson, Collins, 1977.

Coral Reef, Jump! Nature Book, Franklin Watts, 1991.

Coral Reef, Look Closer Series, Barbara Taylor, Dorling Kindersley, 1992.

Coral Reef, Norman Barrett, Picture Library Series, Watts, 1991.

Coral Reefs: A Global View, Les Holliday, 1989.

Coral Reefs and Islands: The Natural History of a Threatened Paradise, William *Sea Trek,* Martha Holmes, B.1. C. Books, 1991.

Grey, David and Charles, 1993.

Reef, Land Shapes Series, Brian Knapp, Atlantic Europe, 1992.

Seas and Oceans, Habitats Series, Ewan McLeish, Wayland, 1996.

Seas and Oceans, David Lambert and Anita McConnell, Orbis, 1985.

The Great Barrier Reef, Isobel Bennett, Lansdowne.

The Greenpeace Book of Coral Reefs, Sue Wells, 1992.